Animals That Live in the Tundra

Musk Oxen

By Roman Patrick

Gareth Stevens
Publishing

Please visit our Web site, www.garethstevens.com. For a free color catalog of all our high-quality books, call toll free 1-800-542-2595 or fax 1-877-542-2596.

Library of Congress Cataloging-in-Publication Data

Patrick, Roman.
 Musk oxen / Roman Patrick.
    p. cm. – (Animals that live in the tundra)
 Includes index.
 ISBN 978-1-4339-3903-7 (pbk.)
 ISBN 978-1-4339-3904-4 (6-pack)
 ISBN 978-1-4339-3902-0 (library binding)
 1. Musk ox–Juvenile literature. 2. Tundra animals–Juvenile literature. I. Title.
 QL737.U53P38 2011
 599.64'78–dc22

                                            2010002250

First Edition

Published in 2011 by
Gareth Stevens Publishing
111 East 14th Street, Suite 349
New York, NY 10003

Copyright © 2011 Gareth Stevens Publishing

Designer: Michael J. Flynn
Editor: Therese Shea

Photo credits: Cover, p. 1, back cover Thomas Kitchin & Victoria Hurst/First Light/ Getty Images; pp. 5, 7, 9, 11, 13, 21 Shutterstock.com; p. 15 John Dominis/ Time & Life Pictures/Getty Images; p. 17 Photos.com; p. 19 Paul Nicklen/ National Geographic/Getty Images.

Printed in the United States of America

CPSIA compliance information: Batch #CS10GS: For further information contact Gareth Stevens, New York, New York at 1-800-542-2595.

Table of Contents

Boldface words appear in the glossary.

Hairy and Smelly!

What is big, hairy, smelly, and lives in the **tundra**? A musk ox! The musk ox is named for its special smell called musk.

Male musk oxen are called bulls. They may weigh as much as 800 pounds (360 kg)! **Female** musk oxen are called cows. They are a bit smaller.

All musk oxen have large heads and short necks. Two sharp horns dip down on either side of a musk ox's head. Bulls have long horns. Cows have shorter horns.

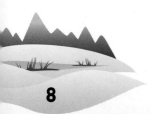

horn

Two Coats

A musk ox wears two coats in winter! Musk oxen have long, dark hair as their outer coat. A short wool coat lies under it. These coats keep musk oxen warm.

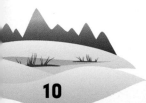

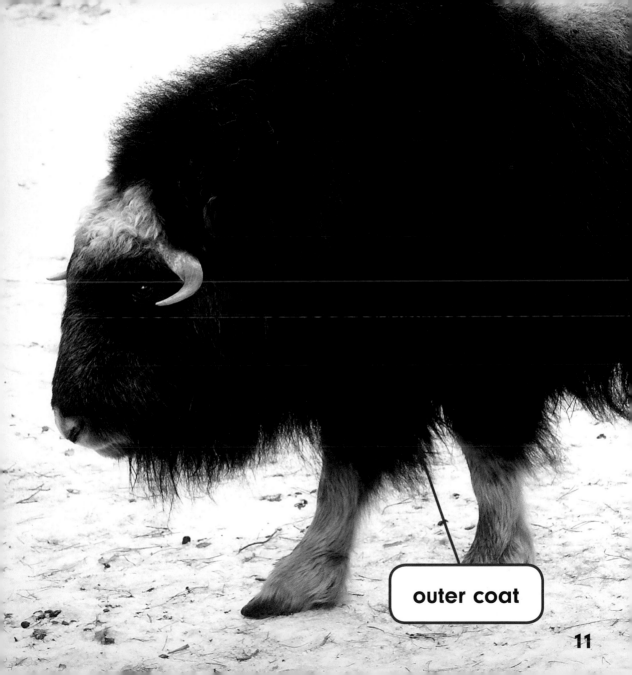

outer coat

In spring, the tundra gets warmer. Musk oxen **shed** their inner coat. When winter returns, musk oxen grow their inner coat again.

shedding inner coat

13

All Together Now

Musk oxen live in herds. Often, one cow is the leader of the herd. The herd eats a lot of plants in the summer. The musk oxen get fat for winter.

herd

In winter, many tundra plants die or are covered with snow. Musk oxen use their hoofs to dig for moss and roots. Their fat helps them stay alive.

hoofs

Arctic wolves and dogs are enemies of musk oxen. If an enemy is seen, the herd **protects** its young. It makes a circle around them. The adult musk oxen will **attack** if necessary.

More About Musk Oxen

Years ago, Earth was colder. Musk oxen lived in many places. When Earth warmed, musk oxen moved north. Today, musk oxen are protected from hunters in some areas.

Fast Facts

Height	up to 5 feet (1.5 meters) at the shoulder
Length	about 7 feet (2.1 meters)
Weight	bulls: up to 800 pounds (360 kilograms) cows: up to 600 pounds (270 kilograms)
Diet	grass, flowers, roots, moss, and other plants
Average life span	up to 20 years in the wild

Glossary

attack: to try to harm

female: a girl

male: a boy

protect: to keep safe

shed: to lose hair

tundra: flat, treeless plain with ground that is always frozen

For More Information

Books

Markle, Sandra. *Musk Oxen.* Minneapolis, MN: Lerner Publications, 2007.

Somervill, Barbara A. *Animal Survivors of the Arctic.* New York, NY: Franklin Watts, 2004.

Web Sites

Animal Diversity Web: Musk Ox

animaldiversity.ummz.umich.edu/site/accounts/information/Ovibos_moschatus.html
This site has many details about musk oxen, their homes, and how they survive.

National Geographic: Musk-Ox

animals.nationalgeographic.com/animals/mammals/musk-ox.html
See a map of the world showing where musk oxen roam. Also, read about musk oxen babies.

Index

About the Author

Roman Patrick is a writer of several children's books. He was born near the Arctic Circle and grew up loving the animals that live there. He now lives in Buffalo, NY.